*Dedicated to José Pérez Montero's grandchildren
and to Anna Johanson*

Little Children's Bible Books
GOD
MAKES THE
WORLD

Retold by Anne de Graaf
Illustrated by José Pérez Montero

SCANDINAVIA

Close your eyes.
Hold your breath. Shhhh.

There was nothing in the
beginning . . . except for God.

God took the darkness and
changed it so that suddenly
. . . there was light.

The light came from
the sun. God made
the earth and moon,
all the planets and
the stars.

10

How many stars? One?
Two? Three? Four? God made
more and more and more and
more. . . .

11

God made the oceans and
the seas. He made more
and more and more and
more fish.

Make your face look like a fish. Whoops! You were asking for a kiss!

13

God made the land. He made more and more and more and more animals.

Which is your favorite? YOU are God's favorite!

God made a man
called Adam and told him to
give the animals names.

What did Adam call these animals?

Then God made a
helper and friend
for Adam named
Eve.

*Just like He made you, your fingers,
your toes, your smile too.*

17

In Eden, Adam and Eve felt
God's love everywhere.

It was like a warm hug waiting for them
wherever they went. Who can you hug?

Adam and Eve
lived in a special
garden called Eden.
There God had made
all different colored
flowers, fish, birds,
animals, trees and . . .

What else?

God had
one rule, not to
eat the fruit from one
tree. God said "no." The serpent
told Eve "yes."

Eve chose to break the rule and so did Adam. This was wrong.

What rules do you know?

27

To listen and do what God wants is the most important thing in life.

Adam and Eve did not listen, so they had to leave Eden. They never, ever felt so close to God again.

God went on loving Adam and
Eve, though. No matter what,
He always loves. God gave two
sons to Adam and Eve.
Every child is a gift
from God.

That means you are a big wiggly present. To whom?

The two sons of Adam and Eve were different. Cain was good at growing crops. Abel took good care of the sheep and goats.

What can you do really well?

One way of saying "thank you" is to give a gift.

Cain gave his crops to God.
Abel offered his best lamb.
God liked Abel's gift better than
Cain's and this made Cain very
angry.

Cain was so mad he chose to hurt and kill his brother Abel.

When we're angry it hurts us and it hurts the people who love us. When was the last time you were mad? Did you say "sorry"?

A NOTE TO THE Big PEOPLE:

The *Little Children's Bible Books* will be your child's first introduction to the Bible, God's Word. In *God Makes the World*, detailed illustrations make the first four chapters of Genesis spring to life. This is a DO book. Point things out, ask your child to find, seek, say and discover.

Pray before you read these stories, that your child's little heart would be touched by the love of God. These stories are about planting seeds, having vision, learning right from wrong, choosing to believe. *God Makes the World* is the first step on The Way. The Bible story is told in straight type.

A LITTLE something fun is written in italics by the narrating animal, to make the story come alive. In this DO book, wave, wink, hop, moo or DO any of the other things the stories suggest so this can become a fun time of growing closer.

Pray after you read this . . . together. There's no better Way for big people to learn from LITTLE PEOPLE.